THE PATH TO GODLINESS

7 INTERACTIVE BIBLE STUDIES FOR SMALL GROUPS AND INDIVIDUALS

PHILLIP D JENSEN
AND TONY PAYNE

 matthiasmedia

The Path to Godliness
Second edition
© Matthias Media 2009

First published 1991

Matthias Media
(St Matthias Press Ltd ACN 067 558 365)
PO Box 225
Kingsford NSW 2032
Australia
Telephone: (02) 9663 1478; international: +61-2-9663-1478
Facsimile: (02) 9663 3265; international: +61-2-9663-3265
Email: info@matthiasmedia.com.au
Internet: www.matthiasmedia.com.au

Matthias Media (USA)
Telephone: 330 953 1702; international: +1-330-953-1702
Facsimile: 330 953 1712; international: +1-330-953-1712
Email: sales@matthiasmedia.com
Internet: www.matthiasmedia.com

ISBN 978 1 921441 38 7

Cover design and typesetting by Lankshear Design.

» CONTENTS

» HOW TO MAKE THE MOST OF THESE STUDIES

1. What is an Interactive Bible Study?

Interactive Bible Studies are a bit like a guided tour of a famous city. They take you through a particular part of the Bible, helping you to know where to start, pointing out things along the way, suggesting avenues for further exploration, and making sure that you know how to get home. Like any good tour, the real purpose is to allow you to go exploring for yourself—to dive in, have a good look around, and discover for yourself the riches that God's word has in store.

In other words, these studies aim to provide stimulation and input and point you in the right direction, while leaving you to do plenty of the exploration and discovery yourself.

We hope that these studies will stimulate lots of 'interaction'—interaction with the Bible, with the things we've written, with your own current thoughts and attitudes, with other people as you discuss them, and with God as you talk to him about it all.

2. The format

Each study contains five main components:

- sections of text that introduce, inform, summarize and challenge
- numbered questions that help you examine the passage and think through its meaning
- sidebars that provide extra bits of background or optional extra study ideas, especially regarding other relevant parts of the Bible
- 'Implications' sections that help you think about what this passage means for you and your life today
- suggestions for thanksgiving and prayer as you close.

3. How to use these studies on your own

- Before you begin, pray that God would open your eyes to what he is saying in the Bible, and give you the spiritual strength to do something about it.
- In the first study, you will read right through Titus to get a feel for its overall content and background. This would be a worthwhile thing to do before each of the remaining studies as well. We won't be studying Titus in verse-by-verse order, so reading it right through before each study will help to keep the flow of the letter in your mind (and it won't take long to read with such a short book).
- Work through the study, reading the text, answering the questions about the Bible passage, and exploring the sidebars as you have time.
- Resist the temptation to skip over the 'Implications' and 'Give thanks and pray' sections at the end. It is important that we not only hear and understand God's word, but respond to it. These closing sections help us do that.
- Take what opportunities you can to talk to others about what you've learnt.

4. How to use these studies in a small group

- Much of the above applies to group study as well. The studies are suitable for structured Bible study or cell groups, as well as for more informal pairs and triplets. Get together with a friend or friends and work through them at your own pace; use them as the basis for regular Bible study with your spouse. You don't need the formal structure of a 'group' to gain maximum benefit.

- For small groups, it is *very useful* if group members can work through the study themselves *before* the group meets. The group discussion can take place comfortably in an hour (depending on how sidetracked you get!) if all the members have done some work in advance.

- The role of the group leader is to direct the course of the discussion and to try to draw the threads together at the end. This will mean a little extra preparation—underlining the sections of text to emphasize and read out loud, working out which questions are worth concentrating on, and being sure of the main thrust of the study. Leaders will also probably want to work out approximately how long they'd like to spend on each part.

- If your group members usually don't work through the study in advance, it's extra important that the leader prepares which parts to concentrate on, and which parts to glide past more quickly. In particular, the leader will need to select which of the 'Implications' to focus on.

- We haven't included an 'answer guide' to the questions in the studies. This is a deliberate move. We want to give you a guided tour of the Bible, not a lecture. There is more than enough in the text we have written and the questions we have asked to point you in what we think is the right direction. The rest is up to you.

5. Bible translation

Previous editions of this Interactive Bible Study series have assumed that most readers would be using the New International Version of the Bible. However, since the release of the English Standard Version in 2001, many have switched to the ESV for study purposes. So, with this new edition of *The Path to Godliness*, we have decided to quote from and refer to the ESV text, which we recommend.

A HELICOPTER JOY-RIDE

[OVERVIEW]

Tucked down at the back of the New Testament, sandwiched between Paul's letters to Timothy and the book of Hebrews, is Paul's short letter to his friend Titus. For many of us it's a book we don't study often, and when we do, it's a bit difficult to know how to apply—there is a lot of very personal and specific guidance for Titus and his situation is very different to ours.

In another sense, however, Titus and his mates were not so different from us at all. They struggled with immorality and error among Christian leaders; they strived to live a consistently Christian life in a world hostile to the gospel; they needed encouraging about the basis and motivation of their lives as well as detailed teaching about behaviour. In other words, though their physical and cultural circumstances were quite

different, their spiritual lives were very similar to our own.

The book of Titus lays before us a *path to godliness*. Though addressed to special circumstances, it gives us some general principles about what godliness is and how we can attain it. We need this teaching now as much as they did then.

Before we look at Paul's letter in detail, we need to take a helicopter ride over it. In this first study, we'll look at some of the surrounding territory (the background information), read Titus right through, and get a feel for its contents and shape.

The story so far...

One good thing about the background to Titus is that it's easy to become an expert. There's not a lot to know. Titus (the man) is not mentioned in Acts, although his name pops up in Paul's other letters as a faithful and honest fellow-worker (e.g. 2 Cor 8:16-23, 12:18). We don't know very much about how Titus came to be in Crete, nor how the gospel first came to be preached there (Paul passed by the island on his way to Rome).

All the solid information we have about the circumstances in Crete and Paul's reasons for writing are contained in the letter itself—so let's read Titus, shall we?

Read Titus 1–3.

Read the following questions and then read right through Titus, answering the questions as you go.

1. What do we learn about the character of the church in Crete:

- the make up of the congregation?

- the past history of the congregation?

- the natural character of the Cretan people?

- the way they became Christians?

- the things that were threatening them?

2. What do you learn about Titus and his role in the church?

3. What do you learn about Paul and his reason for writing?

Passing on the message

MANY FAMILIES HAVE FAMILY traditions or family heirlooms that are passed on from one generation to the next. Whether it is a secret family recipe or a precious piece of jewellery, every generation receives it both as a privilege but also as a duty—they know it will be their job to pass it on to their children one day.

Within the family of God, it is the truth of the gospel and the godly life that goes with it that is passed from one generation to the next. This is what lies behind Paul's letter to Titus (as well as his letters to Timothy). Paul is passionately concerned that the gospel be passed on to the next generation of Christians. People have been converted and churches have been planted, but if the work is to continue and grow, then the next generation of leaders must be equipped to take over. The future of Christianity is at stake.

More than this, Paul sees that the true gospel—the gospel that has been entrusted to him by God (1:3)—is continually under threat, both from a hostile world and from false teachers. As we will discover in our next study, the appointment and behaviour of godly elders (or overseers) is a key element in countering this threat.

The same truth and gospel life that Paul wrote to Titus about are now being passed on to us. It involves a given body of 'sound doctrine', which is only properly understood if it is lived.

» Implications

- What things bind us to the world of the first century? Based on your first reading of Titus, what things do we have in common with the Cretans?

- From your reading of Titus, have a stab at defining what Paul is passing on (in a couple of sentences).

» Give thanks and pray

- Give thanks that God has preserved the truth of the gospel in every generation, allowing it to reach us.
- Ask God to help you to understand the godly lifestyle that goes with the gospel and to live it faithfully so that you might hand on the truth to the next generation.

TEACHERS TRUE AND FALSE

[TITUS 1]

LEADERSHIP IS A SCANDAL IN MUCH of modern Christianity. In the face of an increasingly secular society, many Christian leaders seem either unsure of what their message should be, or incapable of living in accordance with it. Leadership is an important subject in Paul's letter to Titus. As we look at the characteristics of elders and false teachers in chapter one, we will discover significant implications not just for leaders, and for those who appoint leaders, but for the whole nature of Christianity.

An unfinished task

The place to begin this study of Titus is at 1:5 (we'll come back to 1:1-4). Here we have Paul's reason for leaving Titus in Crete in the first place, a summary of Titus' task and Paul's essential reason for writing:

> This is why I left you in Crete, so that you might put what remained into order, and appoint elders in every town as I directed you.

The work of the gospel in Crete needed to be put into order. It was not only incomplete, it was also crooked, and Paul wanted this rectified as soon as possible. This overriding purpose permeates the rest of the letter. Titus was to appoint godly elders to shore up the 'common faith'; but he was also to take a personal role in getting the Cretan church back on the right track—by rebuking, teaching, encouraging, reminding and warning (1:13; 2:1, 15; 3:1, 10).

It is hard to read these words about 'appointing elders' without immediately

Elders and overseers

'Elder' (v. 5) is a translation of the Greek word *presbuteros*, from which we also get the English words 'Presbyterian' and 'priest'. 'Overseer' (v. 7) is the Greek word *episcopos*, from which we get 'episcopal'. (Traditionally, *episcopos* has been translated as 'bishop'.) The use of 'priest' and 'bishop' in some English translations has been particularly unhelpful because these words obscure the meaning of the original words. 'Elder' and 'overseer' have the distinct advantage of being descriptive words that tell you something about who these people were supposed to be—older, wiser, experienced Christians who were qualified to keep an eye on what was happening and act for the good of the congregation.

thinking of our own church structures, with their elders, pastors, presbyters, bishops, priests, deacons or whatever. And certainly, Paul's words to Titus are very relevant to Christian leadership today. However, we must remember that what Paul meant by words like **'elder'** or **'overseer'** may be quite different from how we use the words.

In Paul's mind, there was no difference between an elder and an overseer; they were simply two different words to describe the same animal. (Note how he uses the two words interchangeably in verses 5 and 7.) In the 2000 years since Paul wrote these fairly simple words to Titus, volumes have been written, denominations have split and blood has been shed, all over theories of elder-ship, episcopacy and priesthood. By and large, these theories and the church structures they have spawned, are human in origin and bear all the marks of our human love of power.

For Paul and Titus, however, the theory and practice of elders/overseers was much more straightforward. In the face of opposition and threat, each congregation needed faithful and godly leaders who would stand firm against the opposition and encourage the church. This task is made explicit in verse 9:

He [the elder/overseer] must hold firm to the trustworthy word as taught, so that he may be able to give instruction in sound doctrine and also to rebuke those who contradict it.

There was false teaching present in the Cretan churches and the elders were to play a key role in refuting it and encouraging the Christians to stick to the truth.

Read Titus 1:5–9.

1. What are the marks of a true and godly teacher:

   - in behaviour?

   - in relation to doctrine?

Read Titus 1:10–16.

2. What are the general marks of a false teacher:

   - in behaviour?

   - in relation to doctrine?

3. What were the special characteristics of the Cretan false teachers?

Why does it matter?

You have no doubt picked up the strong contrast Paul draws between godly elders and false teachers, but you may ask: "So what? What's all the fuss about? Aren't people allowed to express a different opinion without being silenced?"

Tolerance (or rather relativism) is one of the hallmarks of our modern Western society. In fact, if Paul was writing these words today, he would no doubt be labelled a 'fundamentalist' in the media. There might even be a campaign on behalf of the false teachers to gain them an equal say in how the church should be run.

Speculation aside, the apostle Paul obviously thought that the false teachers were a very serious problem. He denounces them in the strongest possible terms (see v. 16!). Why did it matter so much to Paul? Here are three reasons.

i. The consequences

The first and most obvious reason for Paul's concern was the havoc being wrought in the Cretan congregation. False teaching is rarely (if ever) an isolated, self-contained or purely intellectual phenomenon. Its consequences are almost always far-reaching and damaging to spiritual health. In this case, the urgent need to silence the false teachers is underscored by the consequences of their teaching—"they are upsetting whole families by teaching what they ought not to teach" (1:11). This had to stop.

ii. It leads people away from God

However, there is another reason that false teaching must be firmly dealt with—it leads people to look for God in the wrong places. In the 21st-century world it is an almost universally accepted idea that there are many ways to God. This modern way of thinking (known as 'relativism') affects even Bible-believing Christians more than we are aware. Whenever we are inclined to think that a particular brand of false teaching doesn't matter too much, or that mutually incompatible theologies can exist comfortably side by side in a congregation, then we betray how much we have been influenced by the mood of our day.

We cannot come to know the true and living God by intuition or by rational thought or by running an experiment or by seeing him on the back of our eyelids. The Bible is quite clear on this—we can only know anything about God because he *reveals* himself to us. Our knowledge of God is not something we have attained through great effort or cleverness—it is entirely God's initiative. We only know what he has chosen to tell us.

For Paul, the importance of revelation formed the basis for his very stern attitude towards the false teachers in Crete. It comes out in his opening greeting and description of himself. Let's take a look at it.

Read Titus 1:1–4.

1. Paul sees his ministry as being for "the faith of God's elect and their knowledge of the truth". What is the result (or accompaniment) of this faith and knowledge? Where does it lead?

2. What is this faith and knowledge based on?

3. God has promised all this, but where do we hear this promise? How is it made known?

4. How does all this help explain Paul's attitude to the false teachers?

iii. Teachers are important

IF CHRISTIANITY IS BASED ON A revealed message, sent from God, which promises eternal life and leads to a life of godliness, then we can see why true and godly teachers are so important.

Think about it for a minute. Our hope of eternal life is based on the promises of God—a set of promises that was revealed through the life and death of a first-century Jew called Jesus and subsequently entrusted to his apostles. It is absolutely vital, therefore, that the promises of God are maintained from generation to generation. They must be defended and passed on faithfully, because our whole relationship with God (our faith and knowledge and godliness) is based on these promises. False teachers are *the* enemy because they destroy this true knowledge of God by distorting the given message. We can begin to see why Paul was so concerned about the Cretan situation, and why the doctrinal maturity of the elders was so important.

If the gospel that has been entrusted to Paul leads to a life of godliness (v. 1), then we can also see why the *behaviour* of elders is so significant. Not only does it model the lifestyle, which all Christians should pursue, but it demonstrates that the elders have truly understood the message that they are supposed to protect and proclaim. True knowledge of God leads to godliness; that is its very character. If we think we have grasped that knowledge and yet there is no godliness in our lives, then we are self-deluded— we have not grasped the message at all, and we are certainly in no position to teach and lead others.

The ungodly behaviour of the false teachers damns their teaching, for behaviour and doctrine are inextricably bound together. Bad behaviour reveals an underlying ignorance of God; and bad behaviour also distorts the message, as we seek to rationalize and justify our lifestyle.

As Paul looked to the future, he saw the fundamental importance of sound doctrine and godly living for the survival of the young churches under his care. We neglect this twofold emphasis to our peril.

» Implications

(Choose one or more of the following to think about further or to discuss in your group.)

- Why is it important that we know our teachers and can see their lives?

- In appointing leaders (whether for congregations, youth groups, beach missions or Sunday school classes), what personal qualities should we look for?

- What characteristics do we often look for instead?

- Although this passage speaks directly about elders (true and false), what does it tell us about the lives of all Christians?

- What does this passage stir us to pray for?

» Give thanks and pray

- Think of some of the issues that have been raised in the study. Discuss and pray about them in your group, or individually.
- Pray for the Christian elders/overseers who teach you the Bible. Pray that they would strive to be true and godly teachers, always teaching sound doctrine.

>> STUDY 3

MOTIVATION FOR A CHANGED LIFESTYLE* [TITUS 2:1-15]

BEING A CHRISTIAN MUST AFFECT the way we live. We sense that this is so, almost instinctively, and we cringe when Christians (especially those in the public eye) act as if this is not the case. The Christian hypocrite, whose mouth says one thing but whose life says another, is an object of derision.

Even so, working out just how our knowledge should affect our behaviour can be confusing. There are times when 'Christian' behaviour seems indistinguishable from 'non-Christian' behaviour (both would agree, for example, that stealing is wrong); and there are other times where we are at odds with our non-Christian neighbours (e.g. over sexual morality). And when Christians fail to live by their profession, or seriously water it down, it muddies the waters still further.

The apostle Paul was convinced that knowledge of God should lead to godliness (1:1-2). In fact, this was one of his primary concerns about the church in Crete. The Cretan national character did not provide the best pattern of life to have been raised in and the Cretan Christians (under Titus) needed to grow and develop into changed people; people who were to "devote themselves to good works" (cf. 1:12-13, 3:14).

However, we need to be aware of two possible problems as we approach this whole subject: legalism and licence.

* Keen observers may notice something odd as we proceed through this study: we have missed out Titus 2:1-10. This has been a deliberate move. We will look at the *motivation* for a godly lifestyle (in Titus 2:11-14 and 3:1-8) before filling out the *content* of a godly lifestyle (in Titus 2:1-10 and 3:9f.).

Being good?

This is perhaps the single greatest misunderstanding of Christianity in our community. Many people believe that Christianity is all about, or mainly about, morality; that it's about what you *do*. For many people, being Christian has nothing to do with a commitment to Jesus and to knowing and following him, it's just about being morally respectable. If you are a decent, upstanding member of society, then you are seen as being a Christian. Christianity becomes equivalent to the accepted social moral order and has nothing to do with listening to Jesus.

Religious legalism

A more 'religious' version of legalism tries to *add* things to our basic trust in Jesus. In Paul's day, he was confronted by a circumcision club who thought that it was necessary for all Christians to rigorously obey the Jewish law as well as put their faith in Christ for forgiveness. In our day, we see this among some sub-Christian sects who require certain patterns of obedience in order to earn salvation. And we see it among some mainline Christian groups when they insist that certain practices done in certain ways (e.g. baptism, the Lord's Supper) are *essential* for our salvation.

Problems

i. Legalism

Legalism takes a number of forms: e.g. the widespread perception that **'being good'** equals 'being Christian'; or the **religious** form of legalism, which seeks to *add* things to our basic trust in Jesus. Legalism is disastrous in all of its forms because it attacks the cross of Christ. Paul wanted the Cretans to lead a changed lifestyle but he didn't want to lay a new law on them. He didn't want to say to them, "You need to do this and this and this in order to be saved".

ii. Licence

The second, and opposite, problem is licence. This is the view that since we are completely forgiven through Christ's death, how we live doesn't really matter. If there are no laws hanging over our heads, then we are free to do as we please. We are free to indulge ourselves, because we can always go back to God for forgiveness if the need arises.

Paul was not too impressed with this 'blank cheque' style of Christianity. He didn't want legalism, with its carrot-and-stick approach to life, but neither did he want the Cretan Christians to think that they could simply live as they pleased. Paul knew that it *mattered* how you lived, but he had a problem: how do you move a donkey without a carrot or stick?

The answer is in Titus 2:11-14, which we will now study in some detail.

Read Titus 2:1-14.

1. The word 'for' links verses 11-14 with the verses before it. What do you think is the significance of this word?

2. The word 'grace' is well-known in our culture as a religious word. It has many meanings, ranging from an incantation said before meals to a way to address holy persons ('your grace'). Here, in Titus, it carries its usual biblical meaning, which is something like 'generosity'. Grace is undeserved, unmerited favour— in this case from God. See if you can think up an illustration or an event from your life that illustrates the concept of grace.

The grace of God is said to do two things in this passage: it brings salvation to all people (v. 11) and it teaches or instructs us (v. 12). Let's look at each of these in turn.

Grace that saves

3. 'Salvation' is another religious word. It simply means 'rescue'. It is perhaps stating the obvious, but before someone can be rescued, they need to be in some sort of danger or trouble. Is there any indication in verses 11-14 about what it is we've been rescued from?

4. According to Titus 2:11, "the grace of God has appeared, bringing salvation for *all people*". This could conceivably mean:

  a. the whole of humanity
  b. all kinds of people.

Given the context of this verse (coming straight after verses 1-10), which of these two options do you think Paul meant?

5. Looking through the rest of our passage (vv. 11-14), what 'appearing' do you think Paul is referring to? Give reasons for your answer.

6. How did this salvation take place? How was it done? (Try to put it in your own words without any jargon.)

7. What was the underlying purpose of the rescue?

8. What are the implications of this understanding of salvation for:
- the legalism problem?

- the licence problem?

Grace that trains

9. The grace of God that has appeared is also said to go on teaching or training us. It doesn't just save us and then leave us to carry on with life as before. It trains us to live differently. *How* do you think this might happen?

10. What two things will it train us to do? Expand on what you think each of these things mean.

11. How does this new way of living affect our relationship with:

- ourselves?

- other people?

- God?

The path to godliness

IN OUR LAST STUDY (ABOUT TEACHERS true and false), we saw that there is a close connection between *knowledge* and *behaviour*. The true message from God leads to godliness, and we can recognize false gospels because they do not yield a godly lifestyle. That connection is reinforced in Titus 2:11-14.

The grace of God that has saved us through the death of Jesus also trains us in how we should live. If we have received this generosity from God—if it has released us from slavery and purified us to be worthy of belonging to God—then our lives will be different. As we wait for Jesus to return (v. 13) and as we call to mind all that he has done for us, we are motivated to say 'no' and 'yes'—no to all that drags us back to our former slavery; and yes to the way of life that we were always meant to live, the way of life that puts us both in control of ourselves, and in right relation to others and God.

When we are caught in a current about 100m off the beach and the life-saver appears and drags us onto his surfboard, what happens next? We don't ask to be thrown back in; nor do we expect to spend the rest of our lives on the board. We head for the beach to begin a new life, a life in which we might be more careful about where and how we swim. Our salvation is not an end in itself. It is but the first stage in a whole new life, a life lived for God rather than for ourselves.

» Implications

- Do you know this grace of God we have been talking about? If so, how has it changed the way you live?

- Our motives are often hard to untangle, and we should not expect to achieve complete purity of motive until heaven. Given this, what different motives do you think lie behind the way you live at the moment?

- Which of these should you try to change?

» Give thanks and pray

- Give thanks to God for the appearing of his grace in Jesus.
- Ask God to keep teaching you by his grace to live out the purpose of your salvation (be specific in bringing areas of your life that need attention to God).

WHY BORN-AGAIN CHRISTIANITY IS AUTHENTIC [TITUS 3:1-8]

WHEN WAS THE LAST TIME YOU described yourself as a 'born-again Christian'?

I'm willing to bet that you can't remember, either because it was about 20 years ago or because the words have never passed your lips. It's not a title we like to go by these days. It conjures up images of tub-thumping evangelists with lots of teeth (and lots of money). It's a plastic, phoney kind of expression in our society, often spoken in jest with a slight southern accent ("Ahm borrn agin").

There are no doubt many reasons why people don't like born-again Christianity, but it is curious that many Christians also find the term just a little objectionable. It is, after all, a very biblical way of speaking (Jesus was not embarrassed to use it in John 3). What is it about 'born-again' that we don't like? Here are four suggestions.

i. It's hypocritical

We have seen too many religious phoneys who go by the name 'born again' to be very fond of the words. For example, American politicians seem to adopt the 'born-again' tag to secure the (substantial!) Christian vote. They start attending church and going to prayer breakfasts just in time for the presidential race to start.

ii. It's threatening

Many people prefer Christianity to look like Doris Day did in some of her movies —shot with a soft lens so that the edges are blurred. This sort of 'blurred-again' Christianity is much easier to cope with than the rather abrupt, absolutist born-again variety. It's more comfortable, especially for fence-sitters.

To claim to be born again is to make a

fairly stark and threatening sort of claim. It implies that you have made a whole new start—that you are the genuine article. It exudes an air of confident self-identity. It says, "I am in and you are out".

This threatens people, both Christians and non-Christians. The non-Christian feels alienated, and finds such a sharp, picket fence difficult to sit on. But Christians, too, can feel uneasy about the whole subject—how can I be sure that I am one of the true born-again Christians and not a counterfeit?

People don't like born-again Christianity because it is threatening.

iii. It's arrogant

Being born again also seems to imply a degree of arrogance. If I label myself 'born-again' then it seems that I'm claiming to be better than you. Born-again Christianity conveys a holier-than-thou sort of impression.

This is especially so for the many people in our society who equate being Christian with *being good*. If Christianity is all about morality, then surely the genuine, true-blue, born-again Christian is claiming to be especially good. And because we suspect that they aren't that good, we label them an arrogant hypocrite.

iv. It's immoral

Others complain that being born again seems like a licence to do whatever you like (see our comments on 'licence' in study 3). If being a Christian means starting from scratch and having everything forgiven (being born again), then what motive is there for morality? It's not only unjust that immoral people should be given a clean slate like that, but it discourages others from doing their best. Or so it is argued.

Why born-again Christianity is authentic

Despite these objections, we need to come to terms with the fact that being born-again is an authentic, biblical way to describe what it means to be a Christian. It is historically authentic, in that the term is found in the original documents of the New Testament on the lips of Jesus, Peter, Paul and James. But it is also theologically authentic (as we shall see) because it describes something of the essential nature of becoming (and being) a Christian. Jesus went so far as to say that "unless one is born again he cannot see the kingdom of God" (John 3:3).

Let's look at our passage and see what it tells us.

Read Titus 3:1-8.

1. In order to gain a feel for how this short section flows, fill in the following summary of verses 3-8. (Complete each phrase from the passage and briefly explain it in your own words.)

   - We were once...

   - But God...

   - not because...

   - but according to...

   - by the...

   - so that...

2. Verse 2 talks about showing "perfect courtesy toward all people". How do you think this relates to the verses that follow?

3. How should the massive change or new start that is described in this passage affect the way we live?

PAUL'S DAZZLING DESCRIPTION OF born-again Christianity turns many of our perceptions upside down. According to Paul, being born again, or 'reborn', is not an arrogant proclamation of how good we are, but a stunning admission of how enslaved and foolish we once were and how miraculously and undeservingly we have been changed. God has scrubbed us clean, drenching us with his Spirit, to make us worthy heirs of his kingdom.

However, at least one of the charges people bring against born-again Christianity is true: it is threatening. If becoming an heir of eternal life is only achieved through this radical transformation of 'rebirth and renewal', then we start to do something that other people hate. We start to draw lines. We say, in effect, that those who have not tasted this saving act of God, are foolish, deceived and enslaved, as we once were (v. 3). This will not win us friends. As Paul says elsewhere, those who are outside of Christ find the gospel a terrible stench to their nostrils. Those who are being saved find it the sweetest of all smells (2 Cor 2:14-16).

There is only one brand of Christianity, the original one taught by Jesus and his apostles. New Testament Christianity is about a total transformation of sinful people through the merciful power of God. That's born-again Christianity, and it's the real thing.

» Implications

(Choose one or more of the following to think about further or to discuss in your group.)

- How might this understanding of the Christian life affect our prayers? What would it lead us to pray for?

- Why do some people find the message of God's grace offensive? What is it about the message that gets under our skin?

- Why should being born again make you truly humble rather than arrogant?

- Would you say that your own life is marked by perfect courtesy to all?

- Why should being 'reborn' minimize hypocrisy rather than promote it?

- Why should being 'reborn' lead to morality rather than immorality?

» Give thanks and pray

- Give thanks to God for giving us new birth in spite of what we were like.
- Pray for the courage to be distinctive in the right way, even though this will be offensive to some people.
- Ask God to continue to help you to be courteous and humble.

>> STUDY 5

THE CONTENT OF A CHANGED LIFESTYLE [TITUS 2:1-10]

WITH THE SORT OF PAINFUL clarity that only advertising can achieve, the billboard said it all: "This month in [Magazine X], the complete guide to success in career, health, sex, finance, beauty, travel and much, much more".

We can only wonder what the "much, much more" included. Certainly, it is hard to think of a more apt summary of all that our society wants—'lifestyle' is everything. We don't just want to exist— to be born, consume and die—we want the 'good life' (whatever that is). Our whole social structure is based on this constant desire for a higher or better standard of living. Governments rise and fall on their ability to deliver it; we work all our lives in order to attain it (if not for ourselves, then at least 'for the kids'); and businessmen and advertisers grow fat by persuading us that their particular products are an essential part of attaining the perfect 'lifestyle'.

This desirable lifestyle is defined for us in all kinds of ways. We watch our parents and learn what is worth (or not worth) striving for. We absorb values in the classroom, in the workplace, at the pub, and especially in the blue light of our TV screens.

Christianity is also about a lifestyle, one that has its own particular content and motivations, and often stands quite opposed to what the rest of our society thinks of as the good life. In our last two studies, we looked at the motivation for a Christian lifestyle. In this and the following study, we'll start to fill out the content of Christian living, as we find it in Paul's letter to Titus. To put it another way, we have looked at the start of the path to godliness, and the forces that keep us moving forward; now we'll look at the content of godliness that we're striving for.

Read Titus 2:1-10.

1. Look back over studies 3 and 4. Summarize the motives that lie behind a Christian lifestyle.

2. What other motivations can you find in Titus 2:1-10? Can you see any connections between knowledge/doctrine and godliness?

3. In Titus 2:1-10, Paul follows a favourite first-century practice of describing the way people should live in terms of a 'household code' (for other examples see Ephesians 5; Colossians 3; 1 Pet 2:13-3:7). He works through the key social relationships and describes the appropriate Christian behaviour for each group.

   Write down the things Paul directs Titus to teach each group and note any areas that you don't understand.

   • Older men

   • Older women

- Young women

- Younger men

- Slaves

The perverse unpopularity of the Christian

AS WE WORK THROUGH GOD'S guidelines for a 'good' life, we're struck by how appealing and yet how unpopular these values are. In many respects, our non-Christian society is strangely attracted to these values. Who would not want older men to be sober-minded and dignified, self-controlled and showing wisdom and love? Who could not but be drawn to the idea of a devoted, pure young woman who has been taught to love her husband and children by an older, wiser woman? Who would not want workers to be respectful, hard-working and trustworthy? Who would not respect a self-controlled, upright young man?

Our society longs for a set of values like this and yet, perversely, when confronted with them, refuses to live this way. And when Christians try to live this way, we are ridiculed. We find ourselves in conflict with our work-mates when we choose to act honestly when they are all abusing the system. We are often scorned by our peers when we choose purity over decadence, and uprightness over shame. We are pressured on all sides to go with the flow, to adopt the same materialistic, selfish lifestyle as our neighbours, to sacrifice our family lives to the gods of achievement, money and job satisfaction.

Paul's 'household code' proposes a radical alternative lifestyle, motivated by the grace of God in Christ and defined by what pleases God. Making this lifestyle our own will draw us into conflict with our non-Christian world at various points and we need to be ready for it. But if God's grace has entered our lives, it will keep teaching and urging us to face that conflict, reject ungodliness and exercise self-control.

›› **Implications**

(Choose one or more of the following to think about further or to discuss in
your group.)

- Which of the groups in Titus 2 do you fit into? What is God telling you to do
  here? (Be specific and practical.)

- Perhaps the most controversial of Paul's directions concerns young women.
  To suggest that young women should be "working at home" and "submissive
  to their own husbands" is hardly popular in our society. It is in areas like
  these that we find the clash of values most severe.

  - Do these verses forbid a woman from working in a job outside the home?

  - What principles or values about family life are being taught here?

- From verses 3-5, would you say that loving your husband/children comes easily and naturally?

- 'Self-control' features prominently in this passage (in fact, for young men, it is a blanket statement that seems to cover everything). What does our society think about self-control? In what areas do you find self-control difficult? (Be honest.)

- How might modern, secular values affect your godliness:
  - at work?

  - with your family?

  - at church?

» Give thanks and pray

- Give thanks to God that Christianity brings with it a whole new lifestyle.
- Ask God to help you with particular areas of godliness that you need to be working on in light of Titus 2.
- Pray for those who might be ridiculing you for your way of life. Ask God to challenge them to take the claims of Jesus seriously. Ask God to give them new birth.

» STUDY 6

THE PATH TO GODLINESS

[TITUS 3:1-15]

I N OUR LAST STUDY (TITUS 2:1-10), we began to look at the content of a Christian lifestyle. We saw that Paul wanted Titus to instruct the people to live godly lives in accordance "with sound doctrine" (Titus 2:1). In this study we'll continue to think about that content by looking further at chapter 3. This is fairly straightforward material, but it requires us to think seriously about our lives.

In Titus 2:1-10, we saw Paul's 'household code' for the different social groupings in the Cretan church. In chapter 3, he talks about their behaviour as citizens and as members of the congregation.

Read Titus 3:1-3.

1. As the Cretan Christians relate to the world around them, what kinds of things should mark their behaviour?

2. How does this behaviour contrast with what they were once like (and presumably what their neighbours are still like)?

3. Which of these areas of life is particularly difficult for you? Why?

Read Titus 3:4-14.

4. In their relationships with each other as a church, what should the Cretan Christians avoid? Why?

5. Given that not all disagreements are wrong (e.g. in chapter 1 the elders were to have some arguments in order to silence the false teachers) what are some ways of deciding whether something is a pointless controversy or an important argument?

6. What will it look like to be devoted to good works (v. 14)?

7. Do you think others would describe your life like this?

The path to godliness

Titus 3 is a deceptively simple chapter. It is not hard to understand what Paul is asking people to do. Submitting to authorities, being gentle and patient and avoiding foolish arguments are all relatively straightforward commands. It is tempting to whip through these chapters without doing the hard work of allowing them to challenge our lives. In some ways this is the hardest chapter of Titus, because it requires us to acknowledge our failings and to repent and seek God yet again. But if we have understood the rest of Titus properly, then this is where we are taught by the grace of God to say no to ungodliness and yes to self-controlled lives. Make sure you take the time to reflect prayerfully, personally and deeply on your own life in the light of these words.

» Implications

(Choose one or more of the following to think about further or to discuss in your group.)

- As we relate to our world, what things make it difficult for us to be submissive to authorities, to be gentle and to avoid quarrels?

- What implications do these verses have for Christian social or political activism?

- Why do we find controversy and argument so attractive?

- What issues today might fall into the 'unprofitable controversy' category?

- What does verse 14 teach us about the purpose of good works?

» Give thanks and pray

- Ask God to keep equipping you to be able to discern between important arguments about the truth and foolish controversies.
- Pray for the various authorities that God has placed over you (the government, the police force etc.) that they will be wise and just.
- Pray for Christians in countries where the authorities are particularly unjust. Pray that your brothers and sisters in Christ will be able to submit appropriately to those authorities.

RE-TRACING THE PATH

[REVIEW]

PAUL'S SHORT LETTER TO TITUS, even though written in a time and place far removed from our own, teaches us important things about living as Christians. It teaches us that Christianity is not simply a body of doctrine, nor merely a code of morality. It is a relationship with God, initiated and established by God, based on a true knowledge of him, a knowledge that leads to a radically changed life.

This is the path to godliness. It is a simple path, yet a narrow one, for it avoids the errors that are so prevalent in our time. It does not diminish the crucial importance of sound doctrine (as so many do today), and neither does it drive a wedge between what we know and how we live (as many others also do). It keeps the two bonded tightly together. True knowledge of God is the basis for godliness. If we do not have godliness, then we have not understood the knowledge of God; and conversely, if we don't know the truth about God, we have no hope of pleasing him and participating in the eternal life he has promised.

We've looked at these things (and more) over the last several weeks and now is the time to try to pull it all together.

Read the whole book of Titus.

Now close your Bible and see if you can answer the following questions. This is not a test—there are no marks or certificates. These summary questions are designed to help you review what Titus is about and to entrench it in your mind.

1. Where was Titus?

2. What had Paul left Titus to do?

3. What two words describe the leadership ministry to which Titus was to appoint people?

4. What were the sorts of characteristics that Titus was to look for in suitable people for this ministry?

5. Why is it so important for teachers to display godliness of life?

6. What is the result of true Christian knowledge?

7. What is the motivation for a changed lifestyle?

8. What is 'grace'?

9. What two things does 'grace' do?

10. In Titus 3:5, we are told that God saved us:

- not because...

- but according to...

11. What will be our attitude to others (i.e. other sinners) if we have been reborn through God's mercy?

12. How do Christians receive the Holy Spirit?

13. Summarize the Christian lifestyle of:

- the older man

- the older woman

- the younger woman

- the younger man

- the slave

14. Summarize how Christians should relate to the non-Christian world.

» Implications

- What things would you like to give thanks to God for as a result of working through Titus?

- What key areas of life have you been challenged in as a result of reading Titus?

» Give thanks and pray

- Give thanks to God and pray in light of your answers to the two implications questions.

> ### Feedback on this resource
>
> We really appreciate getting feedback about our resources—not just suggestions for how to improve them, but also positive feedback and ways they can be used. We especially love to hear that the resources may have helped someone in their Christian growth.
>
> You can send feedback to us via the 'Feedback' menu in our online store, or write to us at PO Box 225, Kingsford NSW 2032, Australia.

matthiasmedia

Matthias Media is an evangelical publishing ministry that seeks to persuade all Christians of the truth of God's purposes in Jesus Christ as revealed in the Bible, and equip them with high-quality resources, so that by the work of the Holy Spirit they will:

- abandon their lives to the honour and service of Christ in daily holiness and decision-making
- pray constantly in Christ's name for the fruitfulness and growth of his gospel
- speak the Bible's life-changing word whenever and however they can—in the home, in the world and in the fellowship of his people.

It was in 1988 that we first started pursuing this mission, and in God's kindness we now have more than 300 different ministry resources being used all over the world. These resources range from Bible studies and books through to training courses and audio sermons.

To find out more about our large range of very useful resources, and to access samples and free downloads, visit our website:

www.matthiasmedia.com

How to buy our resources

1. Direct from us over the internet:
   - in the US: www.matthiasmedia.com
   - in Australia and the rest of the world: www.matthiasmedia.com.au

2. Direct from us by phone:
   - in the US: 1 866 407 4530
   - in Australia: 1800 814 360 (Sydney: 9663 1478)
   - international: +61-2-9663-1478

Register at our website for our **free** regular email update to receive information about the latest new resources, **exclusive special offers**, and free articles to help you grow in your Christian life and ministry.

3. Through a range of outlets in various parts of the world. Visit **www.matthiasmedia.com/contact** for details about recommended retailers in your part of the world, including www.thegoodbook.co.uk in the United Kingdom.

4. Trade enquiries can be addressed to:
   - in the US and Canada: sales@matthiasmedia.com
   - in Australia and the rest of the world: sales@matthiasmedia.com.au

For more resources by Phillip Jensen, go to phillipjensen.com

Other Interactive and Topical Bible Studies from Matthias Media

Our Interactive Bible Studies (IBS) and Topical Bible Studies (TBS) are a valuable resource to help you keep feeding from God's word. The IBS series works through passages and books of the Bible; the TBS series pulls together the Bible's teaching on topics such as money or prayer. As at January 2012, the series contains the following titles:

Beyond Eden
GENESIS 1-11
Authors: Phillip Jensen and Tony Payne, 9 studies

Out of Darkness
EXODUS 1-18
Author: Andrew Reid, 8 studies

The Shadow of Glory
EXODUS 19-40
Author: Andrew Reid, 7 studies

The One and Only
DEUTERONOMY
Author: Bryson Smith, 8 studies

The Good, the Bad and the Ugly
JUDGES
Author: Mark Baddeley, 10 studies

Famine and Fortune
RUTH
Authors: Barry Webb and David Höhne, 4 studies

Renovator's Dream
NEHEMIAH
Authors: Phil Campbell and Greg Clarke, 7 studies

The Eye of the Storm
JOB
Author: Bryson Smith, 6 studies

The Beginning of Wisdom
PROVERBS VOLUME 1
Author: Joshua Ng, 7 studies

The Search for Meaning
ECCLESIASTES
Author: Tim McMahon, 9 studies

Two Cities
ISAIAH
Authors: Andrew Reid and Karen Morris, 9 studies

Kingdom of Dreams
DANIEL
Authors: Andrew Reid and Karen Morris, 9 studies

Burning Desire
OBADIAH AND MALACHI
Authors: Phillip Jensen and Richard Pulley, 6 studies

Warning Signs
JONAH
Author: Andrew Reid, 6 studies

On That Day
ZECHARIAH
Author: Tim McMahon, 8 studies

Full of Promise
THE BIG PICTURE OF THE O.T.
Authors: Phil Campbell and Bryson Smith, 8 studies

The Good Living Guide
MATTHEW 5:1-12
Authors: Phillip Jensen and Tony Payne, 9 studies

News of the Hour
MARK
Authors: Peter Bolt and Tony Payne, 10 studies

Proclaiming the Risen Lord
LUKE 24-ACTS 2
Author: Peter Bolt, 6 studies

Mission Unstoppable
ACTS
Author: Bryson Smith, 10 studies

The Free Gift of Life
ROMANS 1-5
Author: Gordon Cheng, 8 studies

The Free Gift of Sonship
ROMANS 6-11
Author: Gordon Cheng, 8 studies

The Freedom of Christian Living
ROMANS 12-16
Author: Gordon Cheng, 7 studies

Free for All
GALATIANS
Authors: Phillip Jensen and Kel Richards, 8 studies

Walk this Way
EPHESIANS
Author: Bryson Smith, 8 studies

Partners for Life
PHILIPPIANS
Author: Tim Thorburn, 8 studies

The Complete Christian
COLOSSIANS
Authors: Phillip Jensen and Tony Payne, 8 studies

To the Householder
1 TIMOTHY
Authors: Phillip Jensen and Greg Clarke, 9 studies

Run the Race
2 TIMOTHY
Author: Bryson Smith, 6 studies

The Path to Godliness
TITUS
Authors: Phillip Jensen and Tony Payne, 7 studies

From Shadow to Reality
HEBREWS
Author: Joshua Ng, 10 studies

The Implanted Word
JAMES
Authors: Phillip Jensen and Kirsten Birkett, 8 studies

Homeward Bound
1 PETER
Authors: Phillip Jensen and Tony Payne, 10 studies

All You Need to Know
2 PETER
Author: Bryson Smith, 6 studies

The Vision Statement
REVELATION
Author: Greg Clarke, 9 studies

Bold I Approach
PRAYER
Author: Tony Payne, 6 studies

Cash Values
MONEY
Author: Tony Payne, 5 studies

Sing for Joy
SINGING IN CHURCH
Author: Nathan Lovell, 6 studies

The Blueprint
DOCTRINE
Authors: Phillip Jensen and Tony Payne, 9 studies

Woman of God
THE BIBLE ON WOMEN
Author: Terry Blowes, 8 studies

By God's Word

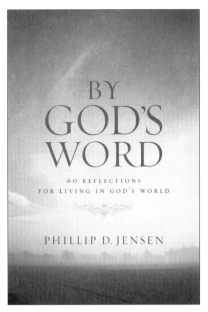

The Scriptures are the glasses by which we bring the world into focus. When we look through the glasses of Scripture, we see God and his world and his people and ourselves more clearly. There are some things, especially about God, that we would never see at all without the Scriptures. There are many things about the world, others and ourselves that we would see in a completely distorted fashion without these glasses. The word of God changes our perspective.

Each week for the last few years, internationally renowned preacher and evangelist, Phillip Jensen, has written a short essay for the congregations he serves at St Andrew's Anglican Cathedral in Sydney, about living in God's world, from the perspective of God's word.

By God's Word is a collection of 60 of the best of these essays or reflections, which offer warm encouragement to live by God's word in every aspect of our lives: from prayer to politics, from forgiveness to fatherhood, and from drought to democracy. Each reflection is also followed by a Bible passage for further thought and reflection.

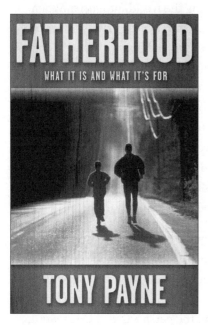

Pathway Bible Guides

Pathway Bible Guides are simple, straightforward, easy-to-read Bible studies, ideal for groups who are new to studying the Bible, or groups with limited time for study.

We've designed the studies to be short and easy to use, with an uncomplicated vocabulary. At the same time, we've tried to do justice to the passages being studied, and to model good Bible-reading principles. Pathway Bible Guides are

simple without being simplistic; no-nonsense without being no-content.

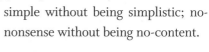

As at February 2009, the series contains the following titles:

- *Beginning with God* (Genesis 1-12)
- *Getting to Know God* (Exodus 1-20)
- *One Life Under God* (Deuteronomy)
- *The Art of Living* (Proverbs)
- *Seeing Things God's Way* (Daniel)
- *Fear and Freedom* (Matthew 8-12)
- *Following Jesus* (Luke 9-12)
- *Peace with God* (Romans)
- *Church Matters* (1 Corinthians 1-7)
- *Standing Firm* (1 Thessalonians)

FOR MORE INFORMATION OR TO ORDER CONTACT:

Matthias Media
Telephone: +61-2-9663-1478
Facsimile: +61-2-9663-3265
Email: info@matthiasmedia.com.au
Internet: www.matthiasmedia.com.au

Matthias Media (USA)
Telephone: 1-866-407-4530
Facsimile: 330-953-1712
Email: sales@matthiasmedia.com
Internet: www.matthiasmedia.com

The Daily Reading Bible

The all-in-one, take-anywhere package to help you feed regularly from God's word.

This popular devotional series is becoming the staple diet for many Christians as they spend time with God. *The Daily Reading Bible* is an all-in-one resource and a good way to get started or keep going in your daily reading of the Bible.

Each volume contains around 60 undated readings. Each reading is designed to take around 15-20 minutes, and contains:

- the full text of the Bible passage
- questions to get you thinking
- 'points to ponder'
- ideas to get you started in prayer.

It's all together in one booklet that you can take with you anywhere—on the train, on the bus, to the park at lunchtime, or to your favourite armchair.

Vol	Contains studies on...
1	Matthew 5-6, Joshua, 1 Corinthians 1-4
2	1 Corinthians 5-7, Malachi, 'The Trinitarian God'
3	Genesis 1-11, 2 Thessalonians, Hebrews 1-7, 'Jesus, the Coming One'
4	Matthew 8-16, Nehemiah, Hebrews 8-13
5	James, 'The Atonement', Genesis 12-35
6	Ephesians, Lamentations, Proverbs
7	1 Peter, Zechariah, Revelation 1-3, 'Present Suffering'
8	John 1-12, Hosea, 'Words and the power of what, how and why we speak'
9	John 13-21, Isaiah 1-12, Philippians
10	1 Timothy, Exodus 1-18, 'The Christian calling'
11	2 Peter, Genesis 36-50, Ecclesiastes
12	'Elijah', Matthew 1-4, 1 Thessalonians
13	Luke 1-6, Amos, 2 Corinthians
14	Luke 7-9, Micah, Galatians
15	Luke 9-15, Jonah, 2 Timothy
16	Luke 16-19, Job 1-26, 1 Corinthians 8-16
17	Luke 19-24, Job 27-42, 'Church'
18	Acts 1-9, Numbers, Colossians
19	Titus, Isaiah 13-27, The Ten Commandments
20	Judges, 'Practical Christian Living', Daniel

FOR MORE INFORMATION OR TO ORDER CONTACT:

Matthias Media
Telephone: +61-2-9663-1478
Facsimile: +61-2-9663-3265
Email: info@matthiasmedia.com.au
Internet: www.matthiasmedia.com.au

Matthias Media (USA)
Telephone: 1-866-407-4530
Facsimile: 330-953-1712
Email: sales@matthiasmedia.com
Internet: www.matthiasmedia.com